Energy Machines

Inquiries should be addressed to Raintree Publishers Inc., 205 West Highland Avenue, Milwaukee, Wisconsin 53203.

Library of Congress Number: 79-27714

2 3 4 5 6 7 8 9 0 84 83 82 81 80

Printed in the United States of America.

Library of Congress Cataloging in Publication Data

Ackins, Ralph.
Energy machines.

Includes index.
SUMMARY: Discusses various machines involved in finding, processing, transporting, and distributing such types of energy as solar, gas, oil, coal, wind, and nuclear. I. Title.
TJ163.95.A24 621.4 79-27714
ISBN 0-8172-1336-8 lib. bdg.

Photographs appear through the courtesy of the following:
American Gas Association: cover, pp. 4, 7, 10, 11, 12, 13, 14, 15 16, 17, 18, 19
Department of Energy: pp. 9 (bottom), 24, 25, 26, 27, 28, 29, 30
FMC Corporation: pp. 5, 6, 8, 9 (top)
Gulf: pp. 20 (inset), 21, 22, 23
Elizabeth Zerbe: p. 3
Sohio: p. 20

energy MACHINES

Ralph Ackins

RAINTREE CHILDRENS BOOKS
Milwaukee • Toronto • Melbourne • London

Millions of years ago sunlight fell on swamps. Plants and animals got energy from the sun. Then the plants and animals were buried. After thousands of years, they changed into what we call fossil

fuels. Coal is the most abundant fossil fuel. When coal is near the surface of the earth, it is strip mined. Giant earth-moving machines strip away the soil. This uncovers the coal.

But after the coal is taken away, the land is scarred and cannot be used. Coal companies try to return the land to the way it was before it was mined. This is called land reclamation. These two men are checking plant growth where there was once a strip mine.

When coal is deep in the earth, it is mined from underground. There is a machine to help with each step of coal mining. There are machines for blasting, cutting, drilling, and carrying the coal away. The roof of a coal mine must be held up securely. Otherwise a cave-in could be a danger to the miners' lives.

The biggest users of coal are steel mills and electric power plants. Steel mills use coke, which is made from coal. Electric power plants burn coal to make steam. This steam runs turbines, and they generate electricity. Coal can be turned into gas by heat and pressure. This is done at a gasification plant, like the one on the right.

Natural gas is a very important fossil fuel. It was formed in the same way that coal was. Gas supplies about one-third of the energy used in the United States. To find gas, scientists study land and rock formations on the surface and underground. Gas is also found beneath the oceans. Crews of people work on special platforms on the water.

Because it is expensive to drill for natural gas, scientists must be as sure as possible about finding the gas. Gas is found in only 14 out of every 100 wells that are dug. Drillers usually have to dig from 1,000 to 18,000 feet (305 to 5,500 meters).

A well that produces gas is called a gasser. The equipment used to drill for gas is called a rotary rig. When gas is found, it flows through drill pipes. To control the on-and-off flow, a master valve is installed at the head of the drill pipe. Above this is a network of pipes and valves called a Christmas tree. The Christmas trees on the opposite page are used to control the flow of gas into gathering lines.

The two men are checking valves on the gathering lines of a natural gas field. From these gathering lines, the gas will go to cross-country pipelines. Most of the natural gas in the United States is found in the southwest. To get this gas to the rest of the country, 260,000 miles (418,430 kilometers) of pipeline were constructed. That is farther than it is from the earth to the moon!

Natural gas must be cleaned before it can be used. The scrubber towers on the left do this job. The machine below is called a dehydrator. It removes water from the natural gas. The gas is stored underground for future use.

Natural gas can also be stored in liquid form. Liquid gas takes up much less space. Natural gas has to be cooled to many degrees below zero to become liquid. The gas storage tank on the right is keeping liquid natural gas cold. Gas that is not stored goes to users. It arrives from a pipeline. Gauges such as the ones below measure this flow of gas through the pipeline. The gas next reaches a city gate station. From the control center, which has computers, the gas goes to houses, schools, hospitals, and industry.

At the city gate station a chemical is added to the gas to give it an odor. That is because natural gas has no odor. And it would be very hard to notice a gas leak without this odor.

A service pipe connects the main gas pipe used in the city to the smaller ones in your home. This gas travels through a meter. The meter tells the gas company how much gas has been used.

Natural gas is a popular fuel. It causes less pollution than coal. It is more efficient than electricity. Natural gas is not found everywhere in the world. Some countries buy gas from other countries. A special tanker is used to carry liquid natural gas.

Supplies of fossil fuels will someday run out. Other ways of finding energy must be explored. Kelp, which is a seaweed, can be converted into gas energy. The kelp is grown, harvested, and then dried. The dried kelp can be burned to produce methane gas. Burning plant material to get energy is called bioconversion.

Oil is a very expensive fossil fuel. It is a nonrenewable source of energy. This means that once the supply of oil is gone, it will be gone forever. About one-fourth of the world's oil supply is in the Middle East and North Africa. North America and Russia each have about one-sixth of the world's supply. The United States uses more oil than any other country.

Getting oil from beneath land or ocean is very much the same as getting natural gas. Oil is often found with natural gas. Machines similar to the rotary rig are used. Sometimes a pump is used to help keep the oil flowing.

Before oil can be used, it is processed in a refinery. First the crude oil is heated in a furnace. Gases form and are carried up a chimney. These gases are collected. Then they become liquid. Some products made this way are gasoline, kerosene, and fuel oil. When fuel oil is reheated it forms diesel oil, lubricating oil, asphalt, and paraffin wax. The most important oil product is gasoline. Oil products are sent around the country in tanks on trucks and trains.

WRNX 121
Gulf

Sunlight is plentiful and free. It can be turned into solar energy. But sunlight is difficult to collect. One way to do this is by using glass. Glass absorbs sunlight. Part of the light turns into heat. The rest is reflected. The heat can be used to boil water to make steam. The steam can run turbines. This produces energy. Solar energy is used to heat homes and schools. It can also be used to help irrigate farm fields.

Wind has been used for centuries to do work. At one time wind was the only source of power to move ships across water. Windmills were invented about 1,000 years ago. They were used to pump water and grind grain.

Windmill-like machines today may be used to make electricity. These machines are called wind turbine generators. Wind turns the blades of the mill. The blades turn a generator. And the generator makes the electricity.

Another source of energy comes from heat that is trapped underground. This is called geothermal energy. Geysers are forms of geothermal energy. So are volcanoes and hotsprings. A well is dug to capture this energy. The water and steam from these wells can run turbines, which make electricity.

The largest solar energy storehouse is the sea. The energy is collected by using an Ocean Thermal Energy Conversion (OTEC) power plant. A chemical liquid is turned into vapor from the heat of the ocean water. This vapor has enough pressure to turn a turbine.

Some energy comes from nuclear power plants, right. Here atoms are split, creating energy.

The machine below is called a fusion power reactor. Here atoms are combined, creating energy. Fusion reactors are still being tested. But they should be safe for the environment and people.

GLOSSARY

bioconversion	The process of burning plant material to make energy.
Christmas tree	A machine that controls the amount of gas that goes into gas lines.
coke	A fuel that is made from coal. Coke looks like coal but is much harder.
dehydrator	A machine that removes water from natural gas.
fossil fuel	A fuel such as coal. Fossil fuels come from plants and animals that changed their forms after being in the earth thousands of years.
gasification	A way to change coal or oil into gas.
gasser	A gas well that actually produces gas.
gate station	The place that takes gas from a pipeline and sends it to the users.
gathering line	A gas line that collects gas that comes from wells in a gas field.
geothermal energy	Heat energy that is under the earth. Geo means "earth." Thermal means "heat."
land reclamation	The restoring of the land of a strip mine to the way it was before the mine was made.
OTEC	Ocean Thermal Energy Conversion. A way to collect the sun's heat energy from the ocean.
pipeline	A line that carries gas or oil to various parts of the country.
refinery	A factory where oil is processed so that it can be burned as a fuel.
rotary rig	A machine that is used to dig oil or gas wells.
solar energy	Energy that comes from the sun's light and heat.
strip mine	A coal mine near the surface of the earth. Huge strips are dug in the earth, and the coal is then scooped up.
turbine	A machine that changes one kind of energy (such as steam) into another kind of energy (such as electricity).
wind turbine generator	A machine that changes wind power into electricity

INDEX